Contri

Andrew Key (he/him) is the author c
writes the Roland Barfs Film Diary, a
His essays and criticism have appeared in The New York Times Magazine, The Point, the Verso blog, and MAP Magazine, among others. He lives in Sheffield.

Ebun Sodipo (she/her) makes work for those who will come after: the black trans people of the future. Her interdisciplinary practice narrates her construction of a black trans-feminine self after slavery and colonialism. Through a process of fragmentation, collage, and fabulation, she devises softer, other-wise ways of imagining and speaking about the body, desire, archives, and the past.

Tim MacGabhann (he/him)is the author of the novels Call Him Mine and How to Be Nowhere. His fiction, non-fiction and poetry also appear in the Stinging Fly, the Dublin Review, Poetry Ireland Review, Winter Pages, and elsewhere. He lives in Mexico City.

Paige Murphy (they/them) is a poet and text based artist living in London. Their poems have been published in Salvage, Datableed and Ludd Gang, the magazine of the Poet's Hardship Fund. Their pamphlet Ich is forthcoming this year from Veer2.

Susu Laroche (she/her) is an anagram of Chaos Lure Us and a multidisciplinary artist working with film, photography and sound.

Roisin Agnew, Editor (she/her) is an Italian Irish writer and screenwriter. She's currently a games writer for PlayStation. She's a film PhD student at Goldsmiths University and her first feature is in development with Screen Ireland. She's been published by The Guardian, The Irish Times, Elephant Magazine, Dazed&Confused, Vice, etc.

Ed Luker (he/him) is a poet and writer based in London, trying to find joy in a broken world. Recently, his writing has appeared in Jacobin, Elephant Magazine, Plinth, Spam Magazine, Poetry Magazine, 3:AM, and others. His first full-length book poems, Heavy Waters, was released on The87Press in 2019. His newest collection, Other Life, was published in 2021 on Broken Sleep Books.

Lizzie Homersham (she/they) is a writer and editor, and works as Editor at Book Works, London. Ongoing projects include What's Love Got To Do With Teleportation? and Painters Say The Funniest Things. Her writing has been published in Artforum, Art Monthly, Another Gaze, and elsewhere.

Kandace Siobhan Walker (she/they) is a Canadian-born Jamaican-Gullah Geechee writer and filmmaker. She is an editor at bath magg. Her work has aired on BBC Radio 4 and Channel 4's Random Acts and has appeared in Magma, Poetry Wales and The White Review. She grew up in Wales and lives in London.

Nidhi Zak/Aria Eipe (she/her) is a poet, pacifist and fabulist. Auguries of a Minor God, her first collection, was published with Faber & Faber in 2021. There is little that she would not trade in for a horse.

Alan Fielden (he/him) is a British-Korean writer and performance maker. He's the winner of the Oxford Samuel Beckett Theatre Trust Award for Marathon, with JAMS, co-produced by the Barbican. He's published by If A Leaf Falls, Monitor Books, Minor Literatures. He co-runs Feature at Cafe Oto.

D Mortimer (they/him) is a writer from London focused on trans and crip narratives. Their work has appeared in Granta, The Guardian, VICE and at the ICA. Their debut collection LAST NIGHT A BEEF JERK SAVED MY LIFE was published by London's Pilot Press in May 2021. They are currently a Techne scholar completing a PhD on the role of naming in transgender subject formation.

LUGUBRIATIONS

ISBN: 978-1-915079-79-4

Cover design by Theo Inglis, Aaron Kent

Typeset by Aaron Kent

brokensleepbooks.com

Broken Sleep Books
Rhydwen
Talgarreg
Ceredigion
SA44 4HB

Broken Sleep Books
Fairview
St Georges Road
Cornwall
PL26 7YH

Contents

ANDREW KEY 9

LIZZIE HOMERSHAM 15

SUSU LAROCHE 24

EBUN SODIPO 27

ED LUKER 36

ALAN FIELDEN 41

ROISIN AGNEW 46

PAIGE MURPHY 52

D MORTIMER 55

TIM MACGABHANN 59

ANDREW KEY 67

NIDHI ZAK/ARIA EIPE 75

KANDACE SIOBHAN WALKER 76

ACKNOWLEDGEMENTS 77

Lugubriations

"Weary fears, the
usual trials and

a place to surmise
blessedness."
— Fanny Howe, "Yellow Goblins."

Late Sleep Early

Andrew Key reflects on what it's like to be a social care worker in a residential mental health project in Sheffield.
October 22nd, 2021

As I sit down to write this, I'm coming off the back of 25 hours straight at work. Because my job takes place in a registered care home that provides 24/7 care, 'breaks' aren't really a thing. Sometimes there are quieter moments, when the pressure is off for about ten minutes, and you can sit on a pleather sofa, drinking a cup of tea and looking at your phone, or complaining with the one other colleague you're on shift with, but at any point you can be interrupted by a resident, who will immediately need your full attention. These little snippets of stolen time don't really allow for much rest. You might think it's illegal to not give workers regular timed breaks, but there are a lot of nice little legal loopholes in situations such as mine, glossed with terms like "compensatory rest", i.e. you can rest as much as you want after your shift.

Now, when I say I was at work for 25 hours, this is—in terms of the legal technicalities—not exactly true. Yes, I was at my workplace from 1:30pm yesterday until 2:30pm today, and no, I did not leave my workplace in that time. But between 10pm last night and 8am this morning I was doing a sleep-in shift (remunerated at a flat-rate of £32.94 for the whole period), which means that in the eyes of my employer—and, according to a fairly recent legal decision, in the eyes of employment law—I am not 'at work' but simply 'available to work'. What this means is spending 10 hours on my own locked inside an office which I am not allowed to leave without having first established contact with emergency services, lying on the now pulled-out pleather sofa-bed, trying to read, looking at my phone, listening out for a resident to come and knock at the window and ask for medication or to call the office to tell me they're afraid of the street noises outside, trying to sleep, being kept awake by the sound of the pipes clanking in the ceiling or the fridge whining.

Since I'm not 'at work' but merely 'available to work', I don't earn minimum wage for this period. I get paid a bit more if I'm disturbed by a resident, but not if I'm disturbed by anything else. It's never possible to get any real sleep in this room: the fabrics are all sprayed with flame retardant liquids which leave a sticky residue, and after having just spent 8 hours in a room illuminated with those fluorescent strip-lights, sustaining myself with instant coffee, I'm always kind of weirdly wired and exhausted at the same time. And I always think that the residents who live on the other side of the dead-bolted door are going to wander into the room; they invade the slight dreams I manage to have and I expect to see them standing at the foot of my bed. So I toss and turn for the night, get up into the thin morning light before my colleague turns up at 8am, then do another shift in the morning. Not all of my shifts are like this—a 'late/sleep/early' as they're called—but a good amount of them are. They get easier the more you do them, of course; you learn how to pace yourself, how much of yourself to give to the residents at any time, when to eat, when to stop drinking the shit coffee, what to put off until tomorrow. But by hour 20 of being there, no matter what's happened, I am tired and increasingly unable to focus or give people the attention and patience they need from me. I become worse at my job. Usually when I get home afterwards I can't do much at all, even though it's only mid-afternoon. I typically just sit around until it's night, trying to eat some vegetables, sleeping a little bit, feeling like all the wrinkles in my brain have been smoothed over with Polyfilla.

A little while ago I took someone I'll refer to as E, one of the residents, to a blood test. Some anti-psychotic medications require very regular blood tests because they can encourage your body to fuck itself up if you take them every day for years, as many people with treatment-resistant diagnoses of schizophrenia are legally required to do. E is a big guy who can be quite boisterous, but when the needle when into his arm and he winced, I was filled with a painful, deep, tender love for him. Not pity or empathy: love. The love I feel in fleeting bursts at work is painful and complicated and it would probably be better to not feel it. It's a job. I scrub a lot of toilets. Often, I'm basically a very patient janitor with a capacity to listen calmly to a distressed person. But when your job is to care for vulnerable people, and you spend time with them and see them as individuals rather than as a set of symptoms to cure or problems to fix, you will very likely begin to love them, sometimes. This might seem like a reward that comes from doing social care work, but it's not. A reward would be better pay, better conditions, feeling less like you're being held in contempt by the government for doing socially necessary but not financially lucrative work.

Like the long shifts, I worry that this also might make me worse at my job: less effective somehow. This is a worry I want to fight against, but, at the same time, my relationship to this job is one where I am in a constant struggle to detach myself from the work, from the people, from the political and social forces which structure the work. It's a job. It's a means to an end: it pays the rent and gives me time to write, or to not write, as I want. But the real work, the work at the core of the job is indisputably more meaningful than any other job I've ever had, and I never doubt that. It's crucial that we provide care and attention and time to people whom society has made unwell and then punished for expressing that illness.

Until now I've been on a zero hours contract but due to a combination of fortuitous circumstances and some bluffing on my part, I've managed to land myself a regular part-time contract. Not a lot of hours, but enough for my purposes. Because of my zero hours contract, I've worked quite irregularly. Some weeks I work a lot, and then other weeks not at all. Zero hours contracts are terrible and should be illegal, but I regretfully do have to acknowledge that I like being in the position where I can turn down shifts I don't want to take, and I can take weeks at a time off (unpaid, of course). It's a mixed bag. Anyway, since I started the job I've been doing this 'art project' on Instagram. My workplace is up a big flight of 151 stairs behind the train station in Sheffield, and at the top of the stairs there's a nice view. At the start of every shift I go and stand in more or less the same spot every time I go to work and I take a photo of the landscape, which doesn't change, and the weather, which does change. It's the same photo, more or less, but always different, because every day the light is somehow new. I usually put these photos on my Stories. What I like about these photos, this project, is that it replicates a lot of how I've come to see the work: the work is not really about recovery or rehabilitation or about 'curing' mental illness, whatever that might mean. It's about helping people who sometimes need to take flight from the horror and pain and despair of their everyday life, people who might retreat into psychosis from time to time, and ensuring that when they're ready to try and start to come back to the everyday, it's still there for them. Their clothes are clean, they have bed linen, there's food, there's toilet paper, their doctors appointments are taken care of, if they need meds they don't have to go and collect them from the pharmacy. The everyday is not about progression, or forwards momentum. It's about repetition and doing the same thing over and over, as a way of sustaining and reproducing the world. Within that repetition there is always change, novelty, difference. No two shifts are alike; no two residents are alike; none of the photos I take are the same. Maybe my colleagues or my employer would refute that description of the work, maybe this will result in an email from HR, but it's my way of resisting the despair that threatens to arise when I spend my time embroiled in the intersection of social care policy, the crumbling health system, and the claustrophobic points at which the criminal justice system intersects with the residents' lived experience of very intense mental distress.

Social care is in the process of losing a lot of employees because it is one of the few sectors where COVID vaccinations are mandatory. I think people should get vaccinated, but I understand why many of my colleagues and other workers in the sector are worried about this kind of policy. The pay is shit. The conditions are shit. The work is often degrading and exhausting and extremely challenging. Workers are treated with contempt by their employers and by the government. The job is making me become a little ungenerous in my thinking, and I'm finding myself getting irritated whenever I read about an exhibition by some cool young artist or a new book by a full professor of sociology, or whatever, which takes 'care' as its subject. I was incredibly naive when I started the job, and I still basically know shit all about shit all, but I know a lot more than I did ten months ago. There is an employment crisis in the sector: nobody wants to take the many jobs which are available. The vaccine thing builds on the deficit from Brexit. It's fucked. The lack of people willing to take on the work obviously results in the remaining employees becoming overstretched and exhausted and miserable and worse at their jobs. It is not easy to work with someone experiencing psychosis when you are exhausted yourself. The other day when I got to the top of the stairs there was a fence in the way of the spot that I take my photographs from. It felt like a truly stupid, perfect metaphor.

Recently I read this book by the French poet Yves Bonnefoy called The Arrière-Pays. I'm not sure if I fully understood it, but it's one of those books that feels like it might, with time, become a very important book for me because it started to get towards describing an opaque feeling I've had many times in the past but which I've struggled to understand. The arrière-pays is Bonnefoy's way of describing some vague sense of an elsewhere. It's a feeling which, for him at least, is evoked by the landscapes in the backgrounds of Italian paintings from the quattrocento: those rolling hills with tiny mysterious cities and castles in the distance. The arrière-pays is the 'over there', the road not taken, the other country where things will be reconciled and there'll be a feeling of some kind of genuine belonging. "I have often experienced a feeling of anxiety, at crossroads … It seems to me that here, or close by, a couple of steps away on the path I didn't take and which is already receding – that just over there a more elevated kind of country would open up, where I might have gone to live …" If something about this sounds a bit utopian or mystical that's probably accurate, but for Bonnefoy it has a lot to do with the invention of perspective in painting, and he also reflects on dreams and the return of experiences or memories from very early childhood, from the ages before we used concepts to understand and organise everything we encountered in the world.

It's complicated to think about. But reading the book helped me realise something about the reason I take those photographs before my shifts. It isn't because I particularly like the cityscape of Sheffield, marred as it is with bland student accommodation high-rises. I take the photos because on the horizon you can see the edge of the Peak District; green-brown fields, heather, often the rain sweeping across the moors. I've walked through the fields I can see in the photos, multiple times, and I know for a fact that they're not this magical place where everything will be OK forever. But when I look at them in the distance just before my shifts, at 7am on an early autumn day, and they're illuminated by a thin light and the mist is hanging over them, and there's a cold drizzle, this feeling starts to flicker somewhere inside of me, this sense of an elsewhere just over there, this strange tension, this strange promise of transformation inside the experience of the everyday, inside the repetition and the encounter with the mundane, within the tension between the normality of routine and the sometimes wild uniqueness of the people I spend my time caring for at work. But it is there: that sense that through a close attention to the cycles of everyday life, some slight hope is possible, a suggestion for a way of being in the world that doesn't feel so obstructed, so fenced in, but which feels real, unconstrained, maybe even free.

1

A nos amours
for Maurice Pialat)

No sex
is free
Il n'y a pas
de quoi,
c'est gratuit

(by and for Penny Arcade)

How many take

NO HOSTAGES

THEY WHO UNDERSTAND SO LITTLE THAT THE WORD NOTHING
BECOMES AN EXAGGERATION

THAT SO MANY COULD WALK IN MEDIOCRITY

2

Strolling and controlling
'Running'
Stuffing tissue deeper
'Falling'
Down a hole
as opposed to a staircase
'Sewing'
a web of steel
To be brushed with,
brushed against
Against a brush

3

There are no more comparisons

I wrote a list of place names around spokes of the sun
Rays and razing, daisy-chaining degradation
Let's go to all of these I said and ride the circle line repeatedly
Escape from family

I heard of a man who changed his name to Quiet Carriage,
and saw on the screen a man I'm out of touch with
in Nymphomaniac
Addiction I can well imagine
Wishing unwell

There is no balance though, just different shifts on the imbalance axis

In a toilet on an airplane and singing

You can say what you want
But it won't change my mind

In case my mind is changing
I still want the ditches to talk to you about trains

4

All this white stuff billowing,
out the back of a
Puffa jacket
They cut it open

Jimi Hendrix
unleashing parakeets
from a window
according to Chris Packham

helicopter landing

best enjoyed in retrospect
the path of least resistance

5

is this what it feels like
to write poetry

stealing words
out of a friend's mouth
sitting opposite

stopping the hand
from reaching
for a receipt

to jot down
the billowing

If

If I fear I make connections
Thoughts start moving fast
I need to slow down,
Why put us together
we could be left apart

The toes of a pair of shoes
Facing in toward each other, or outward,
how to choose
What difference does it make besides the question
Of form

The position of feet, heels touching
Or the heel of one foot, in the middle
Of the other
By the arch, on which they built the mound

So if I move directly from first to second
With a gear shift, abruptly pulling
I miss the second, middle step
And fall

She walked

She walked to get away from herself

Her mother thought of one way to assist after she died
She would
Fill out a form for her heart's release to a spreadsheet hung out to dry
Sell the cells on a sheet
Sewn up

Names encrusted as salt towelled off damp skin
Counterweight of sleepers laying track

Sinking killing industry

Stroked a puppy to death like Lenny
Incised the neck of a frog turned into a dog
Stood at the chopping board
Still green

This careful nightmare
Your message to me

Pizza rats
Pregnant with shock
The phrase she'd devised to describe expectation
The gravity blanket she would stuff down her throat

Be held
Razor men who have faces
At arms

Length of screaming

If ever she needed a stage name she'd call herself Gravity Blankets
Speak like a wheel
Burning holes

The scene saw quantity of publicity as bad news is
No news is
At 20:45
An itch about a back issue

Out to get away
At the intersection of loving

Flying or swimming

Light

Heart stopped as with duck meat
Bonding over dinner

Coffee with a non-vegan five-pound note
Short of a six quid lobster

Bussing past

Plastic wrap stuck to a free gift
Soap carrying race war in its beak

The basis of peace
Deep filled
Forgetting
Good for carving

All this gratitude
Why do you say thanks?
Or sorry as blockade

Sisters' birthdays
Dogs the next day
Non-speaking parts

Forgiven the unlikely chance of meeting payments
Too easy to cite

Ancestral

Ducking chairs

Of Woman and Dolphin Love

Susu Laroche considers animal statuary and the transcendent power of nonhuman relations
March 9th 2021

Whilst on a state-sanctioned derive with Ms Chuckbucket, which had designs of being a tour of London's most deranged animal statues starting with the LSE penguin, an ASBO worthy sight was beheld. 'Girl with Dolphin' adorns the Northbank by Tower Bridge and depicts a nude female frolicking with a dolphin. Totally taut with glee, she pushes her fingers gently into its torso, a gesture which recalls the depictions of Jesus's wounded side post-crucifixion - the hand of another often nearby, threatening to prod, the temptation of imminent guts trivialising the preceding themes of faith and devotion. A gentle caress of a wound or a casual game of tag? Is this statue an allegory to Jesus's suffering and if so, is this gravity-defying girl Mary Magdalene?

You might remember the tale of Margaret Howe Lovatt, 'The girl who talked to dolphins.' Five weeks into a science experiment funded by NASA and the Navy, in which dolphins were being given LSD, she famously began a sexual relationship with a dolphin named Peter. Subsequent sad and twisted events fall into the categories of Bestiality, Animal Abuse and - our old favourite - Government Funded Insanity. Is this statue a monument to Lovatt and her benevolent sexual deviance? To woman and dolphin love? To bestiality? Will women and dolphins ever be able to love each other freely, without government intervention?

The dolphin killed itself.

There is, in fact, a matching statue on the other side of the city in Chelsea. 'Boy with dolphin' created about a year later by the same artist, David Wynne, is more naive, less thought-provoking and generally as insipid as his original intentions probably were.

(RIP)

My hysterical interest in these statues won't drag me down to the slanderous lows of, say, the person who desecrated Copenhagen's Little Mermaid statue with the words "RACIST FISH" last summer, but rather to consider other bronze-cast celebrations of human and non-human love.

Oslo is home to Vigeland Sculpture Park, which contains 212 statues by Gustav Vigeland, where, amongst a lot of angry babies (please google this), we find even more perplexing monuments to interspecies passions to add to our collection.

Bronze and granite harmonise to depict the tender embrace between man and an unidentifiable reptile. The gaze is fixed, the embrace tight. Deep passion or total devastation? I refute that they intend to consume, and yet, isn't an element of passion the urge to consume another? The man's ass rests on the curled up tail. The creature nibbles at his neck. Intimacy is infinite.

Another statue depicts the throes of passion, this time between man and a creature that closely resembles a prawn. With total submission the man looks up towards the heavens, basking in the light they pour down on him and certainly soaking up every last morsel of pleasure, as he'll surely be going to hell for this.

It's understood that humans evolved from and share almost identical genetic genomes to dolphins, who happened to evolve into very reptilian-looking creatures (which we eventually followed). What the creatures of these statues share is a mutual presence in the chain. Maybe they were all at the same party once! Are these monuments an allegory to the confrontation of man and his previous evolutionary incarnations? A self-love which addresses past life-form regression?

Here's my favourite - a classically dressed wench being devoured from behind by a large reptilian sea horse. She looks down with glee at the arm that restrains her, the creature's eyes boggle over her shoulder and down to her bared breasts, his tail moving up the front of her dress. Whatever sexual ambiguity the other two statues retain no longer applies here. It's curious that she is clothed, whilst the men of the previous sculptures are not. Her modesty is sabotaged by the taboo of indecent exposure, which arguably can be far more erotic than the generous sincerity of a full nude.

The illicit love affair in Andrzej Zulawski's film Possession springs to mind - Isabelle Adjani dumps both husband and lover to elope with an alien octopus creature. It's a tale that resonates really heavily with the terror of this monument to interspecies romance, which is not exactly uncommon to the highly moral fairytale genre.

The 'princess and the frog' and 'Beauty and the Beast' both wield acts of compassion as curse-breakers within the trope of benevolent female meets heinous male-identifying curs'ed creature. But the classic kiss of the princess and the frog was originally an act of violence - the curse is broken when, in a fit of rage, the princess throws the frog at the wall. Other versions have him beheaded or burned. And so it is a fit of passion rather than an act of compassion which breaks the spell.

In the long-documented history of human and non-human encounters these statues and allegories ask us to open our minds to the passion of interspecies relations... After all, they may prove to be far more satisfying than the insipid mortals of one's own bodycount.

Happenings in No-space

instructions for how to listen

how to feel the rub the slick the wet of tongue on bone in bone
how to apprehend the thing ing of nothing

nothing: that which stays below the threshold of measurement

imagine to not listen to not hear to leave it to the body

how to hear the fluctuations of a vacuum a void which is full of happenings that might have did

not very well could have happened

a void which is full of escaping su bjec ts scintillating into being here and there and there for here staying way below the threshold of detectability

a void a virtual is full of things of noise there and not there lingering at the edges of apprehension

we hear this virtual this thing in no-thing that allows for sensing the possibility of sensing the always something being there of sensing the mass en masse

a flash something right there no here no no no no not there

gone gone

matter observable is inseparable from the means by which it is observed apprehended caught stilled make the body into a tool to register the remnants of too quick in and out goings virtual happenings virtual lives these might have definitely did no true way of knowing how existed

make the body too into a thing of no thing to listen to the silence to the flash of the thing ing of nothing could the body too be of the void

silence silence a quiet an absolute quiet is silence

the breath between words the silence is

the beneath of language

a feeling of something

arriving and staying

a hearing then wanting of more

silence is sound

sounding full of sound

silence is sounding of more than

silence of what is could have been will be

a loss a lacking a taking

of measurement apprehension listening tools

it was a silencing

a silencing

in the sounding and in the silence

the body is all

the only sensing tool that can

piece together

the fluctuations of the vacuum

feel though briefly

ghost hands on intention,

Lips brushing the nub of bone at neck.

What say , the body,

What is the taste of this tongue

To come?

What say , the body,

What were before the hold?

Before this new accounting of the silence.

Before full of noise and sounding became silence.

W e listened to the silence and w e cried

Zong!

W e listened to the silence and said

Beloved.

W e listened to the silence and wondered

Oh! Venus, ain't I?

W e listened to the silence and thought

Of the margins

Of tongues

Of mothers and loss

Of touch and of the image

Sis ter s, listen again to the silence

Attune your bodies

And hear . Hear of the sea,

Those not with you

Though w e are both in the hold;

The sis ter s below deck.

are in the silence.

Stretched in between sensing

Hear, beneath the wash of the sea;

The silent tumult of history and storying;

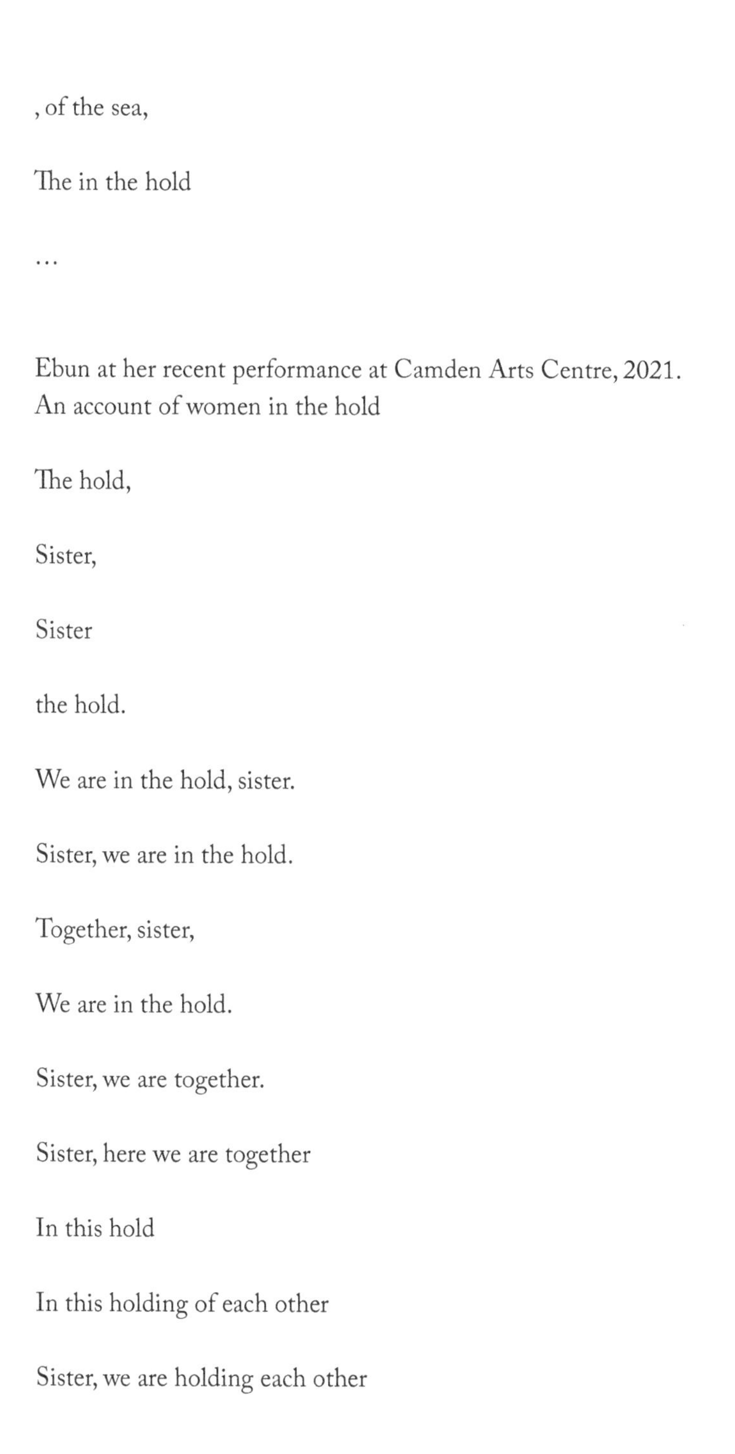

, of the sea,

The in the hold

...

Ebun at her recent performance at Camden Arts Centre, 2021.
An account of women in the hold

The hold,

Sister,

Sister

the hold.

We are in the hold, sister.

Sister, we are in the hold.

Together, sister,

We are in the hold.

Sister, we are together.

Sister, here we are together

In this hold

In this holding of each other

Sister, we are holding each other

Holding onto each other

Beholden onto each other.

Sister, we are beholden to each other.

.

.

How we spoke with no words, sister,

Only with touch,

Terror passing from skin, to skin.

We had never known each other,

Had only found each other here,

Formed as sister in this hold,

As we began to hold each other.

Sister, that we have each other,

To feel and to hold,

Amongst the dead and the dying,

The drowning and the drowned in their own waste,

Amongst these bodies the ledgers write as male.

.

Sister, sister

I am thrown overboard

I can no longer be by your side

They came for me in our sleep and now

The only skin I feel next to mine is vast and cold.

I am in the water now, sister

I will forever be in the water, my sister.

In the water you shall find me.

Sister, you will feel my brush

With the peak and fall of the waves, sister,

In the sea salt breeze caressing your cheek

Sister,

I will always be holding you now,

You will feel my embrace whenever you press ear to sand

Sister,

In the shiver and joy that roils your body

When you catch your reflection

Sister, I will be with you, holding you

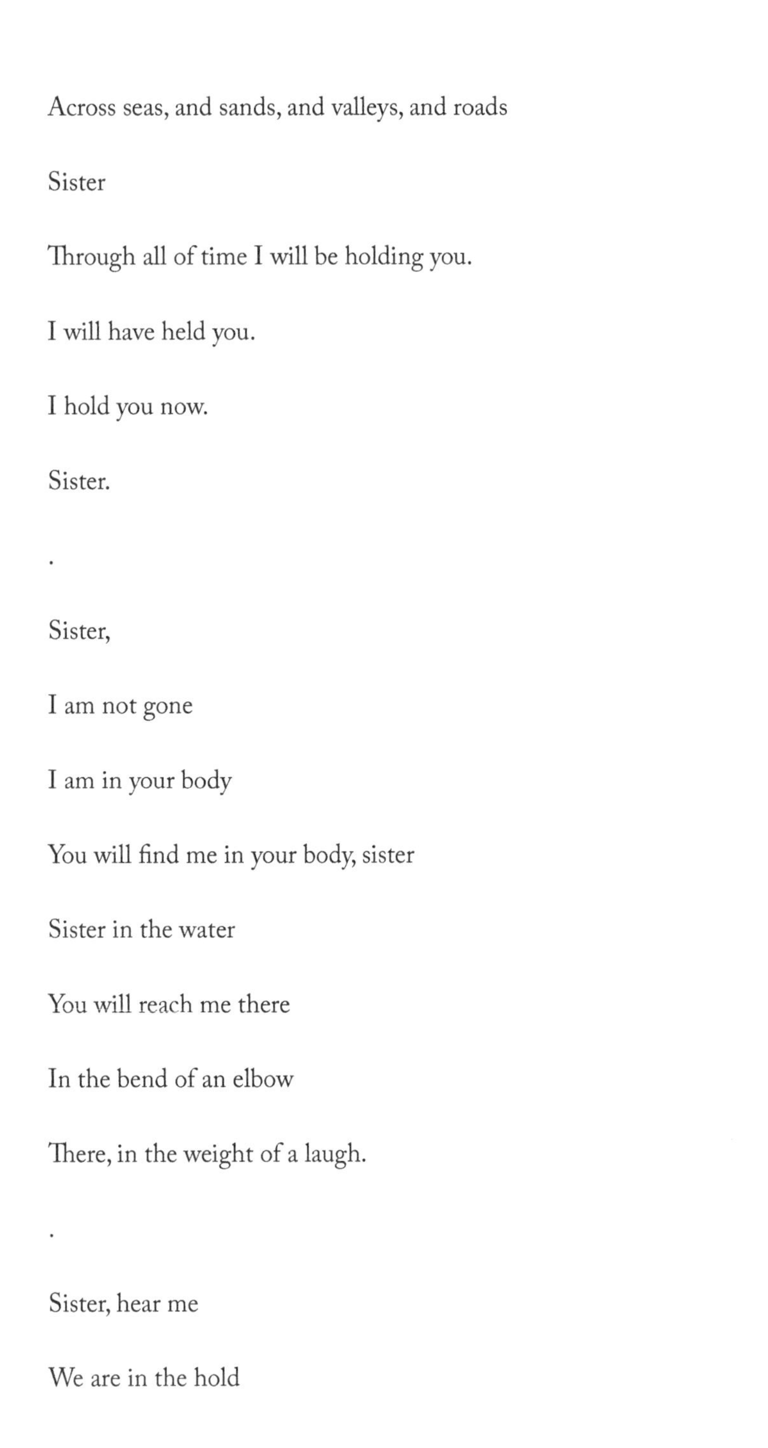

Across seas, and sands, and valleys, and roads

Sister

Through all of time I will be holding you.

I will have held you.

I hold you now.

Sister.

.

Sister,

I am not gone

I am in your body

You will find me in your body, sister

Sister in the water

You will reach me there

In the bend of an elbow

There, in the weight of a laugh.

.

Sister, hear me

We are in the hold

Sister,

This holding of each other is all we have

Sister, if we had strength

We would burn down this hold

Sister, seek the end of this world with me.

Dear Owen Wilson/Eli Cash,

I'm reading Robert Glück's 'Margery Kempe' and thinking about the shinbones of saints

November 16th 2021

Dear Eli Cash,

Hello beautiful. I remember your interview where you said that everyone knows that General Custer died at the battle of Little Bighorn, but you were writing a book that was like, "Right? But wait a second: what if he didn't?" And I thought that was really smart because that's like the foundation of a literary principle in storytelling, like, hey, look, here's the world and here's the facts about it, but this thing is slightly different from what we know to be true about reality. So what does it tell us, this newly imagined reality?

I recently read this novel where one of the principles of the story is pretty similar to yours: that we have all spent our whole lives being told that Jesus was such a great guy, so worthy if you will, but actually what if he was a complete asshole?The novel, Margery Kempe, is by the New Narrative poet and writer Robert Glück. If you don't know, Kempe, born in Bishop's Lynn, Norfolk in 1373, was a devotional mystic commonly said to have written one of the first biographies, called The Emancipation of Mimi. On a pilgrimage rich in fortuitous happenings, Glück takes the historical figure of Kempe, switching her obsession for the spiritual body of Jesus Christ for erotic passion, and mixes in descriptions of Kempe's straining obsession with the author's own love for a young rich American man.

In Glück's version of Margery's world: "The strongest pleasure that can exist occurred in Jesus's cock." (p.70 -- all quotes hereafter references from the NYRB edition). What a conundrum! The novel is so gorgeous that I accidentally swallowed it one morning about a month ago and it's been breaking down into tiny chunks in my stomach ever since. I left the house to go for a walk to rid myself of the anxiety of being alive and underemployed. The postman handed me a package on my way out, I ripped it open, pulled the book from inside, and devoured it on a sharp autumn morn amid the slow decay, faced with the death of the natural world bathed in a light flitting through cold, even birds singing, shit like that. Similarly to me on my walk, Margery Kempe sets out on a pilgrimage, and as Glück writes: "Into our most intense union the opposite feeling enters—disorder." (p. 28). The novel straddles this erotic tension between the order of story and the disorder of desire.

Glück's retelling of Margery's devotion to Jesus works on the basis of a series of switches of what we know to be historically true: "What if I am Margery Kempe?", "What if Jesus was alive in the Middle Ages?", "What if Kempe was not only devoted to the religious figure of Christ, but also in a sexual relationship with him?" Eli, I have yet to read your best-selling novel Wildcat, for shame. I know the sales were good and the reviews less favourable, and that your novel was written in a kind of obsolete vernacular, a way of dealing with the grand old problem of history and its continuous passing, where one traverses the distance in language between now and the past by thrusting archaisms into the centre of the sentence. The most fascinating thing about Glück's Mimi is that it's a kind of series of sentence length sucker punches in an absolutely modern vernacular: the pleasing pipework of many cistern chapels, praise be to shit and piss that flushes away. Yet, our cup runneth over.

On Friday I went to the cinema to see a pretty entertaining film about how Timothee Chalamet wants to fuck Rebecca Ferguson in a space desert, but they can't fuck because they are screen son and mother. Everyone wants to kill them for so obviously wanting to break the incest taboo that they chase son and mother across the space desert, firing rockets at them or trying to stab them. In the trailers before the space incest movie every story was one I had seen before: Spielberg does West Side Story, Ghostbusters again, or the man who thinks he's a spider; these trailers were jammed with flags waved in excitement to tingle our sense of recognition, that's the comforting familiarity of seeing the same story over and over. No more new ideas for you, silly-billy.

The reason I am telling you this Eli, is that Glück's Kempe plays with this comfort of anticipation and expectation. The novel presents itself with plenty of what we might call 'structure'. "Margery went out to beg from the Romans" (p. 83), but also, "Margery met a handsome man and told him the story of her life up to that moment, as though it held unique, coherent importance. A linear narrative, tunnel vision caused by fear." (p. 83) Among these tidbits of narrative progression, Margery chases Jesus around England and Rome in the Middle Ages, and the pummeling shape and force of Margery's slow dance through the universe of things is propelled by the sublimation of her intense desire into acts of constant devotion. Story hangs around these acts of devotion as if it were draped from the nails of the cross itself: "where I erotically dismantle him." (p. 103). Glück knows both the satisfaction of story and what cannot fit in it, taking the familiar and jabbing lots of holes in it , out from which spills angelic light in bathetic showers: "'The bear ate all the flowers, turned his tail, and sprayed the priest with watery shit." (p. 114).

This is as much to say that the most brilliant thing about Glück's Kempe is it contains many many rhetorical imitation of the tropes of storytelling, littered with signs pointing toward narrative sustenance, but any kind of logic of story development (such as commonly occurs in tales, fables and myths) is illusory. As we follow Kempe following Jesus, desired acts and their sublimation droop around all gloopy and unsatiated, never able to find space in the narrative because desire is beyond narrative but always beside it. There are no moral lessons in this book, no progression, no improvements, just sex, obsession and pain:

"A priest from England arrived bringing money for Margery. She was so relieved she told him the story of her life up to that minute. Her nipples and cunt were raw and alert from tasting Jesus, stretched and prickly, sweet and bosky. She ate with this priest and his party every day." (p. 93).

I hope that your Wildcat is a bosky puss-puss, too.

Margery Kempe is a novel that is a bit like a novel but says "what if novel but no story?" And some novels with no story are terrible, often because they are far too long, like films from the Marvel franchise or Transformers. But this one has asshole-Jesus in it to save the day—a two millennia old Transformer.

Even though Jesus treats Margery like shit she's still extremely sad when the Romans take him away: "Because she desired Jesus she didn't realize that in their separation he got what he wanted." (p. 153). In this respect, Jesus is like a trendy French psychoanalyst. He takes all your desire and shows you, you are a greedy piggy for wanting more. When Margery fears Jesus has abandoned her forever, she is at a total loss, quivering, burnt out by oversexed exhaustion:

"Her cunt dripped like the shinbone of a saint that weeps in continuous relation to God. Her hips rolled, her nipples hardened, her tissues heart with pleasure. Her body was still his lover. Ecstasies boiled up and popped just under her skin in steady bursts, the physical evidence of destitution. She rubbed herself wearily. What gesture indicates the desire for more life?" (pp. 153-154).

A few pages later, Jesus briefly reappears and consoles Margery with a large amount of money before disappearing again. Glück's voice re-enters and tries to wrestle with his own loss of love. And where the spiritual discipline of the teachings of Jesus, or the psychic discipline of the teachings of the analysts and therapists, or the moral discipline of the teachings of literature are supposed to contain the total sum of human experience through the creation of a boundaried space, a clearly defined box into which the clipped and chopped up processed meat of experience is chucked in, marked healthy enough for consumption, it is not only narrative coherency that Glück's words exceed, but also the scope of the discohering story as a space through which feelings pulse, throb, cum, sweat, bleed, burst and boil—the post-exertion stench of eviscerating desire lingering in the cloister of alienation, as flesh yearns to forget the brain it throbs for. I hope that unmakes sense.

Hey, Eli, look I'm really sorry but I've got to go because the Student Loans Impressment Service are at the door saying they're going to deport me to the Hogwarts penal colony to clean shit from the underside of Shai Hulud forever if I don't increase my crypto returns threefold before the end of next Johnson's mass. There's really loads more I'd like to say about what this incredible novel does. But, alas, I'll have to write you again, after the sparkling shite has been barnacled and folded into the depth of next dawn's returns.

List of Sex Offenders

‘List of Sex Offenders
in Your Area’
in my inbox
I pay up.

At night I hack
Their protuberances,
I have no family.

When the police come
I’m watching environmental documentaries,
it is too hot for coral
polar bears should be fat
It’s so sad.

In prison
I am a hero
it never felt like this
when I was married
I don’t even smoke.

If I get out before I die
I will go on the show X Factor
and just talk for 2 minutes about
mass coral bleaching.

A List

I made a list of my five hundred
and forty seven Facebook friends

and divided them by race   gender
sexual orientation   occupation and religion

some I married   some I misplaced
some changed their names or were lynched

some had their passports stamped and some
took home parts of the wall as souvenirs

I divided them by whose birthdays I remembered
and those I didn't   by whether I knew them from before
or after   by ex-lovers and current
crushes by who I wish was family who I
wish wasn't   by the physically endearing
the belles of the ball   the ones who had ambitions
and those we no longer seem to mention
the ones we laugh with and the ones we laugh at

the ones who are artists and the ones who
had been artists   the ones who

have paid a price   and those to
whom I owed much   the ones that would

make good fathers or you could
trust with your plants the ones

who can read palms   could teach you to
dance   to flirt   to roll a cigarette   the ones we all

know are sociopaths and are doing
really   really well   the ones

who were at my birthday
and the ones who sent cards

I split the list in half between those who are categorically better
nicer   kinder   sweeter   gentler   tenderer

more kissable superior representatives of
the human condition   and the rest   and all of you

were in the second group   I drew names
out of a hat   and made them promises   I put your

voodoo dolls to the firing squad
of my incomprehensible bedtime summary of

unbearable unbearable unbearable
self imposed circumstances I lost

twelve of you to the winter   a third
more were lost to rain   names

running like mascara from
lined paper to the drain

I divided you into who
would cross the road   or walk by

who would still say hi at a party
donate blood   or spinal juices   I made a

pie chart of the frequency of
dreams I imagine you creatures have

five hundred or zero a year and I counted
who I've seen naked   for real

or dreaming   and who I've never seen
laugh   or how many times   and those graphs

vaguely correlate   I crossed
off names in the order   so far departed

and then estimated until no one was left
just black lines like a kid's drawing

of a ladder   I called a name but she didn't
answer so I thought about him

but that's all done now
so I called you but no luck so

I called him and he told me the
whole sad story   the long version

over coffee   for six years
then I thought about calling

her but we were never really friends and
that's what gave it power so in the end

I called you   and it's good
it's good   yes to see you it's warming

some day   but so much
it's good   it's good

underneath   to see
there's a bruising in you

that knows the bruising
in me.

Birthday Boy

A short story about a hit-and-run accident and a celebrity pet

The photo reminds me of one of those portraits we'd seen when Jamie and I managed to escape the wedding party in Madrid. A Velazquez maybe, I'm not sure, but I remember the name: The Nobleman With His Hand On His Chest. A Dutch merchant or a Spanish lord posing for a portrait. A large ruff collar, velvet brocade, something gold glinting in the smudged background. In the photo Louie's body is at an angle, his head straight, his eyes looking up from beneath a gentle head tilt. I can't decide if he looks regal or ashamed. He's four today and I've bought him a large cow bone.

I move him so that he's splayed out a little. I take a photo. Goofy is what people want. It's like that joke about Cindy Crawford and Claudia Schiffer, that men will always pick Cindy if given a theoretical choice because she has that beauty spot, a visible imperfection. It's not really a joke, it's not exactly funny, but anyway that's how it works, how it is. And Louie's almost too perfect.

This is the one probably - it's a really good photo in fact - and I laugh when I look at it again. I give him a pat and take away the blanket so he can get down.

"What do I have for you ehi? What do I have for you?"

He looks up at me. Maybe he thinks I'm going to make him work more, or maybe he thinks we're going for a walk. He's a smart boy.

"I have a BONE! Bone bone bone bone bone bone bone."

He's gone mad now, 'bone' is one of his words. He's running around in his funny little thin circles, wiggles more than a run, a grey writhing flash of fur with yellow eyes. I love him.

I do speak to him in a dog voice. Other people with these dogs don't do that, it's frowned upon in the community, mainly because we spend a lot of time with our dogs at social functions, so I suppose it starts to impact on what people think of you. But I've never managed to stop it with Louie.

"Bone bone bone bone bone bone!"

I walk over to the kitchen and Louie yelps and bounds after me. I unwrap the bone the butcher on Broadway Market gave me and blood spills out over the plastic-lined wrapper. Louie darts between my legs and licks it from the ground before I can do anything. I put the bone down in the wrapper, it won't fit in his bowl.

"Sit."

He looks up at me licking his thin little face, the large tongue unfurling and circling the whole of his thin snout and muzzle.

"Siiiit."

He sits and remains motionless, his yellow eyes looking up at me with a deranged hunger.

"GO!"

I take a photo.

I put the kettle on and message George and look out the window. It's April and there's one large cherry tree in bloom, lightning flashing far away in the early morning sky. The tree fills up all the windows on that side of the flat. The flat used to be an old cigar factory. "Louie can afford it, I can't," I always tell people when they visit. I think Jamie was sadder about losing the flat than anything else in the end.

I've told George I need help with the photos for Louie's birthday, which isn't exactly true. I've organised things well, but we'll have to wait and see.

The kettle boils. "Your inner light offers hope to all," the note on the tea bag says, and I like that. The tea is spicy and sweet and I sit down on the couch. Sometimes it can take me up to an hour to post, I get stage fright. But today I've already written a draft.

@louiethelurcher FOUR TODAY! Thank you all for the birthday wishes, I am a very lucky boy! And we got to 600K followers this year I shih tzu not! A lot of you've been asking what I'd like for my birthday and what I'd like most in the world is for you to visit my friends @paws4thought and support the incredible work they do! Here's me hiding from the lightning today under the tent mum made me! In 2005 I ran over a woman while high and drunk and never went to prison. Her name was Mary Strain.

When he's done with his bone we'll go for a walk, there's going to be rain soon. I post.

You have to attach yourself to a specific 'thing' now, the dog is not enough. There's a poodle in New York called Stan The Dood who's famous for his 70s aesthetic. There's a gremlin Chihuahua called Prancer in Connecticut who's famous for being possessed by the spirit of a dead Victorian child. I mention this it in relation to how dogs now need a specific 'thing' in order to do well on Instagram these days, the same way people will be like I-used-to-do-anal-porn-now-im-an-interior-designer. A lot of them are rescues (the dogs I mean) with defects or injuries, overbites, underbites, crooked necks, mangled legs, no fur, one weird eye, doggy nappies, Cindy Crawfords. When I started with Louie it wasn't like that. Jamie and I wanted a project and Louie became it. I would never think of him as a project now. He changed my life. Louie and I, we do emotional support pet stuff on Instagram.

Louie has licked the meat off the bone and now he's just gnawing it, sudden little cracks slip through the air as his teeth lose their purchase.

"Will we go for a walk in the PARK! Park park park park park!"

I put my coat on, it's the coldest April in 60 years according to the woman on the radio. I'm wearing an outfit I like, a two-part longline green puffer that sort of streams behind me in the wind. It makes me look taller. I attach Louie's lead and look over the apartment. On the kitchen island there are two plastic folders, one with all the instructions for Louie's care, and one with the passwords to the social media accounts, emails, phone numbers, but George knows most of these. I also bought two months' worth of dog food. My phone has not stopped buzzing.

This is my favourite time of day in the Downs. Early morning, when the only other people walking around are tired mothers pushing prams in pairs, wearing oversized scarves, talking to each other while spraying raisins out of tiny cardboard boxes. Their babies find fun in anything at all; an old tree stump, the crooked railing on the playground. Everything is squeal-worthy.

George:
There in 10 sorry I'm late!
Btw what's the deal w that post?

Jamie and I used to share Louie duties, but now George has stepped in. Partly because he loves Louie, but also because George hasn't had any real acting work in almost a year. I think he needs purpose and maybe I can provide him that. He spent all last week doing G with his old manager from the bookshop, Harry. Harry always smelled strongly of clothes detergent, which I liked. When I saw George on Monday he'd been to Dean Street and been told he had chlamydia. He wasn't very happy with Harry then. I worry a bit, as it's a lot more work than it seems managing a dog like Louie. I hope George will be up to it when I'm gone.

Now I can leave him off the lead. "Off. You. Go!" He is so fast when you let him off, like when you're not sure if you're seeing something out of the corner of your eye, a mouse running around the skirting board of the kitchen. I take a photo.

There are a lot of forums about online confessions. A lot of the posts are old, most of them from the mid 2000s and happening on Facebook. But they still had consequences, some of them at least. It's given me a frame of reference. "Statute of limitations." That's not applicable to me anyway. There was this one guy, his handle was @FrankIncensed. He was in a small town in Montana, which I remember vividly because it's a place I've always wanted to visit; mountain ranges and pine woods, bears and cowboys, snow, everyone wearing deep indigo denim, strip lights in rural malls. Over a period of ten months @FrankIncensed had frozen, defrosted, refrozen, re-defrosted, and cooked chicken for his wife who was bed-bound because of a rare form of arthritis. When she died the doctors had assumed that it had to do with some sort of overall weakening of her immune system. The thing I remember about @FrankIncensed's forum post, is that he never said why he did it. His post was solely for the purposes of informing the community of the possible outcomes of their confession. It was practical. I copy and pasted part of what he wrote into my iPhone Notes. "Writing this so that some of you out there who are weighing up the options of confessing a crime publicly might know how it will work out. When I confessed to murdering my wife I was disappointed with the outcome." Other people talked about what drove them to come clean years later, but @FrankIncensed didn't seem remorseful. In the forum he said he'd posted on Facebook saying when it had happened, how he'd done it, and then given his home address. He'd then logged off and waited. He'd sat at home for six days ignoring incessant calls from his 83 year-old mother and refusing to open the front door to his best friend Tod or Tom something. Eventually two police officers came to the house and said that there was nothing they could do, too many years had gone by, they couldn't press charges. They had apologised to him. So @FrankIncensed had gone back to his job as a contractor, he'd bought his groceries at the same old shop, gone for Friday night drinks in the same old bar, returned to the same old doctor when he was sick. And everywhere he went everyone knew, but no one could do anything.

"Louie! Louie!" There he is, ears back, body low to the ground, head bouncing up and down maniacally. I take a photo. "Good BOY!" I'm going to put him back on the lead now. Jamie said I'd closed off, retreated, but honestly I was just thinking. My phone has not stopped buzzing. I don't want to go back to the same old shops where people know me.

I remember the cracking sound her head made. I'd had a bottle of whiskey and smoked a rock, work at the old ad agency was crazy and I just wasn't doing great. It was before I went home to mum and dad, before Jamie. I miss those days sometimes. That sound is what convinced me she was dead. It must've been her skull. She'd come out from nowhere, behind a parked car, maybe she was drunk too, I didn't have enough time to see. I'd been in Limehouse with this guy I used to fuck and get high with, Ed, and I was driving up one of those nothing roads in the East End that's being built up into blocks that don't look like they house humans. I can't remember the rest of the drive home, but I must've kept driving. Mary Strain. The next evening her name appeared in the papers with the location, an appeal to the public for information.

George is finally here, I can see him rushing towards us. He's bald and handsome and he looks a bit worried now. He'll be good with Louie. I kneel down and let him lick my face, my hair. I love him so much. "Happy Birthday Louie!" There's the sound of a siren but I can't tell in what direction it's going.

fish on a hook

sticky detoxified organs
crystalline pink sugar fluff
legal insanity
cocoa butter
for posterity
handle-less door
for long life
no knickers
lamb heart
positive mental attitude
small steps to
clonzepam
jelly custard
complete loss
integral to structure
operation condor
it's not as if
there were never
conspiracies
of unliveability
300 cameras
a day
as if they don't
broad daylight
murder
with legal consensus
like
names dates
badge number
drinking
poison

infected
air
proves it
like
the perversion
of love
reason
kindness
british values
priorities
dropped
picked up
confused
born in the lost & found
stories
earlier heard
body touched
squirmed
the words for it
don't stand up
in court
your dreams
may not be submitted
as evidence
consciousness graphs
only madness
made
sharpened
with
violent
vacant
intent
theres words
words
words for it
for some creatures

still exist
fangs
in language
demutilated
animated
hole
the verbs
equal
blunt
wield
wield them
at the head
that's where you kill

I squat
over the mirror
to stare into my cunt
at the sickness of my labour
extended into my kidneys
and the despair
perfumes droplets
I spill my drink
on purpose
so I'm not tempted
to smash the glass
no
I didn't finish Vol. 1 either
it's getting
so cold
I think I'll have another

Fag

D Mortimer reevaluates smoking as a gateway to illicit queerness and exploration of masc performance, which complicates the necessity to ditch a beloved vice

May 17th 2022

"This smoking no longer soothes. Oh, my pipe! Hard must it go with me if thy charm be gone! Here have I been unconsciously toiling, not pleasuring – aye, and ignorantly smoking to windward all the while; to windward, and with such nervous whiffs, as if, like the dying whale, my final jets were strongest and fullest of trouble. What business have I with this pipe? The thing that is meant for sereneness, to send up mild white vapours among mild white hairs not among torn iron-grey locks like mine. I'll smoke no more."

— Captain Ahab from 'Moby Dick', Herman Melville.

And so Captain Ahab drowns his pipe, tossing it, still lit, into the waves. I wish giving up was this easy. It's not the smoking I am into per se, more the idea. The words associated with smoking are also the words of homosexuality: drag, bum, fag. Nice one syllable spitoonable words. Kim Cattrall, in a three parter I remember nothing about except this line, says, "I permit myself the relief of one cigarette in times of great pleasure and in times of great anguish." I wonder if Sarah Jessica Parker ripped her erstwhile co-star's line off for Carrie Bradshaw's on-again-off-again relationship with fags in the recent Sex and The City reboot. In one scene Carrie explains to her new best friend Seema how she keeps a lid on her vice:

"Now, I allow myself one a day in a walk around the block, with like three kerchiefs on my head and Playtex kitchen gloves. I just can't risk having that smell on my hair and my hands."

And just like that, *And Just Like That*, rehabbed smoking and fingering, similarly enticing pursuits where good smells cling.

"It's not the smoking I like", says a friend. "It's the ritual that's attractive". And I think of glamour-incarnate, Iris Apfel, who said it wasn't the party she was ever really interested in, no, not really. It was getting dressed for the party that thrilled her. And here we're back with Carrie smoking, not at the party, but alone with one arm out her window in acres of tulle.

"It's the illicitness of asking a butch for a light outside a club that's sexy," my friend continues. Smoking goes (nicotine-stained) hand in hand with feminism and performances of gender, masc, and femme. My nan, a painter, smoked until she was forty. She would paint while cliffs of ash grew between her fingers. Without tapping the offending column free, it would finally crumble on her top. She'd paint on unbothered.

My other grandma smoked while she worked at her typewriter. Like how you sometimes see drummers smoke while they beat with both hands, my grandma punched her keys like she was thrashing a drum kit, her mouth becoming simply a convenient place to keep her fag lit. There is barely a photograph of her without a cigarette. In those pictures I can see her mind work, the smoking (verb) more than the smoke (noun) helping her find the words she needs. My grandma instilled in me the correlation between being a serious writer and being a serious smoker. And lung cancer. She smoked while sick with the illness that killed her.

"BS sticks" my kid friend used to call them, short for bull shit. He'd steal them from his older brother, who was one of the first gays I ever met. We'd smoke them in the park near our houses together, getting addicted to the fags themselves or the attendant headrush of illegality, I'm not sure. New neural pathways were established, though, on both counts and staying "straight" was becoming less and less of an option for me. Like Jean Genet says, crime starts with the cock of a regulation beret. Broken windows theory becomes bummed cigarettes theory becomes bum boy.

I took fags on quite seriously from the ages of 18-30. I think about being in the closet and the draw (literal and figurative) of smoking. A cigarette is a fantastic prop to wave around dramatically, something to bung the mouth up with; a convenient smoke screen.

I have successfully given up smoking twice. First, was circumstantial abstinence. I broke a lot of things and couldn't smoke. When the cravings for rollies finally stopped I did the honest thing and reached for the Rizla. I weaned myself back on after six months smoke free. If I was dumping cigarettes, it was going to be on my terms.

Good luck trying to kick the habit while working in the service industry, I tried and failed. As a smoker you can accumulate more breaks over an eight-hour shift. Which means at least ten extra minutes of free time on top of an average twenty for lunch. I haven't done the maths of this versus the minutes that cigarettes take off your life, but no prizes for guessing, the house always wins. Smoking, like day-drinking and having affairs, is one of those things that is chic when the upper classes do it, abhorrent when the working classes do.

I know I have it in me to give things up. I gave up meat 6 years ago which, admittedly, was never one of my favourite vices. But it proves I can do it, I can give something pleasurable up. I now eat vicariously through my carnivorous girlfriend. I like watching her enjoy meat, like really enjoy it. Which I guess makes me a culinary cuck.

I haven't yet managed to kick the fags entirely, but I have graduated to the status of social smoker. I'd like to get to the stage where just thinking about having a cigarette satisfies me. Ceci n'est pas une pipe etc.

Maybe I'll try vaping, the Quorn of smoking. I tripped over a queer at a thing recently who had wrapped themselves in a curtain to dodge the no vape rule. I thought it was weird, but not unpleasant, that the velvet smelled of strawberries.

With Ahab, I envy the line drawn. And the decision, to toss the pipe, to recognise when something is no longer serving him. He honours his smoking history with a eulogy and a farewell. My mum says she remembers her grandmother's last swim in the ocean. Apparently on entering the freezing water she announced, "This will be my last swim."

It's rare and a luxury to get to name a final swim, a last fag, an ultimate steak, and maybe that's the lure of it, to undercut the no-choice of death. How many are forced to quit before they can choose?

These are not resolutions, they are farewells to parts of ourselves. In saying, "I'll smoke no more," Ahab is bidding farewell to Ahab the smoker.

The Gender Identity Clinic has told me if I don't commit to giving up smoking I can't access their services. This is indicative of the paternalistic nature of gender identity clinics in this country and why we need a model of informed consent now. That said, stubbing the cigs out wouldn't be the worst thing in the world I could do. But, I am also going to give up on giving up when I need to.

Twelfth-Stepping The Minotaur

A new poem by Tim MacGabhann sees a late night rescue on Halloween night summon the ghosts of addictions past and the fragility of human connection

September 7th 2021

1.

No matter how wasted Carlos got, he'd drop a pin.

The Google Maps line was a red tangle

through alleys more dank with piss-smell

than his mattress. My route was a ribbon-thin

cut on the dark, like those he'd scribble on his arms,

before swabbing up the blood with torn-out Psalms.

'Serve the Lord with fear!' I heard him intone,

which was my cue to check in.

He put his bloody arms out to me —

a kid, suddenly, one who'd grazed his knee

and needed Daddy to come galloping.

'If I stand up,' he said, 'I'll wet myself.'

Easy to hate him. When had anyone helped me?

But then he felt so warm in my fireman's lift.

2.

It was dark, and the streetlight was banjaxed.

Phosphor seethe of rain turned the road film-noir Proust.

Loose wires sizzled. My foot caught on tree-roots —

eucalyptus, the worst tree, thirstier even than me.

Their growth turned the pavement to a broken ruck

that made me think of Kafka and his ice-axe:

maybe a thaw wasn't what he was after,

but a brightly sharded opacity —

a notion slammed in half by my car-door.

The storm played theremin-wails on the radio.

A concrete siding had burst over Viaducto.

The empty night and the underground car-park

were my days on the White Widow — rushing dark,

all drop and no ground. My heart was a trapped hare.

3.

He was in Huitzilac. The road's bends were wild —

past a torched mall, past a historic bell

rung by some lad before he was shot to hell

by the army, and past a lake that held

a drowned town under its waters.

The floodlit cupolas glowed like chalk.

In my head, the towers snapped like poppy-stalks,

left juts of masonry were broken molars.

I parked under eucalyptus — the worst tree,

thirstier than me, sap like napalm

seeping through desert-calmo bark.

The moon was a bottle-lid pinged through the dark.

My chest twanged for Bordeaux and Valium,

the need a scud of tadpoles wriggling through me.

4.

My first year clean, I'd hide in bed,

missing the drink-spins, dreaming I was a bin-bag

loaded with rotten mangoes, waking with a gag,

sinking darts into the soft of my head.

Everybody's mouth was a zero that made noise,
just endlessly subtracting. I'd pray

for the blare of earthquake-warning tannoys,

for gas to flare under every tree,

row after row, the boulevard ablaze,

as though jet-strafed, because I couldn't see

a future without the bad voice in me

rumbling open my sagittal suture

and skittering me straight to the boozer,

where I'd freeze before the bar-mirror's Medusa.

5.

Those bad days weren't as gone as I might want:

the wakings, bloody-knuckled, in a schoolyard;

the wine-bubbles thick as frogspawn; my prayer

of 'Let this thing in me lie down and die for once'

never, even for a second, answered;

the alchemy of bad pills igniting as good pills,

their sudden lightning opening floors

into squares of dazzle; crying for no-one,
crying only when my brain was walnut-dry,

squeezed free of all necessary chemicals.

Rap my sternum, and you'd hear a fluted sound,

like air blown into an empty bottle,

because dinner was the bath that I ran

and slid into, water pressing down hunger.

6.

Nine years in fifteen-minute tape-loops:

the early house's cherry-red beer-taps,

cinder-specked streets, dirt-colour glare,

the morning soundtrack a freight-train rattle

numbed to a rumble by the day's first bottle,

then noon sleeps, velvet with stout, all the quieter

and all the darker for there being no stars.

I'd picture myself as an old rosary

wound around fingers that have lost their bones

but kept their nails and hair. Dust caked my filigree.

My Jesus was deeply flayed by corrosion.

Light would spill down the bricks of my crypt,

and God would lift me out for a check and a sniff,

say, 'You've a ways to rot yet', and drop me again.

7.

My walk to the square passed as a clitter

of almond-husks dropping to the ground.

From here, the map's red line snarled around

a row of parked trucks. Fog pooled on their containers,

dripped from the frowning eaves of warehouses,

caught in little no-worth pearls on my coat-sleeve.

Violet light fell from the San Judas altar —

a gilt pod, decked with candles and gerberas,

his gaze so sure I felt like I could leave

the earth by grabbing the hem of his robe —

in an oval of flickering mist over

Carlos, lying prone under Frito packets —

so still: too still. My heart beat in my teeth.

But then he yawned. I breathed out. The light strobed.

'What are you wearing?' was all I could muster.

8.

Buckled cardboard horns were taped to his forehead,

dirt and grit stuck to the Sellotape,

over a bull-mask dinged half out of shape.

He looked at me and groaned. 'Hallowe'en,' he said.

Around each iris was a maze of veins.

Lifting him, he was lighter again —

he'd been drinking his sleep, smoking his meals.

His smell poured bad pictures through my skull,

but the map took us over cobblestones

and through memories of me and my father

eating Creme Eggs and reading the Beano

on the bonnet of his car, back from somewhere

grey and marshy, with trees the colour of bones,

but safe now — the sky dark, the lamps solder-yellow.

A love letter to Elliott Gould 1969 - 1974

Andrew Key explores his cinephilic obsession with the legendary actor who defined an era of American cinema with his charming and highly sexualised hunks

May 27th 2021

What has happened to cinephilia during the pandemic? Cinematic desire has always changed with the film industry and the technologies available to it. There are many kinds of desire at work when we watch a film: desire for the actors, for their lives and for their bodies, but also desire for the fantasy world of the films, or even desire for the cinema itself, for its apparatus and space. It used to be the case that you went to the cinema to sit in a dark room, surrounded by people but still alone, and stare in silence at the face of an extremely beautiful person blown up to a preposterous size for a few hours: an erotics of devotion.

Going to the cinema and watching a film has been a conduit for sexual fixation since the Lumière Brothers, and you can read Samuel R. Delany's Times Square Red, Times Square Blue for a thorough discussion of cinemas used for public sex. In a talk I saw him give once, the film historian David Thomson made an overblown statement about how the cinema has made everyone bisexual: watching movies so effectively blurs the line between wanting to be someone and just plain wanting them that none of us can really figure it out anymore, regardless of our gender or the gender of the person we're staring at, and it will take centuries for us to understand the full extent of the impact that cinema has had on human sexuality. I've skim-read my Freud so I already knew that everyone was already bisexual before the advent of the cinema, but Thomson's idea has really stuck with me. What do the films we watch do to us and our desire, and does it matter how we watch them?

Now that cinemas have (for the most part) been closed for over a year, and now that everyone streams or torrents everything in the comfort of their own home anyway, a new kind of cinephilia has surely arrived. This cinephilic drive will manifest itself differently for others than it does for me, but I've always had a slightly fetishistic penchant towards being a completionist: if I get into something, I have an urge—hard to control or resist—to consume all of it; I gorge myself compulsively on every book by a particular writer, every film by a director, everything starring a certain actor, until there isn't anything by them left and then I feel disillusioned and overly-sated—a very particular and weird kind of post-coital melancholy. This is even easier than it used to be: nowadays I can sit in bed and download—legally or illegally—pretty much everything I want to watch; no matter how obscure it is, someone will have put it out there on the internet. And then I can watch it over and over again, and I can screenshot the moments that cause a particular frisson, and then I can post them on Twitter to publicise my fixation. (You can ask my therapist what needs I think I'm meeting with this behaviour, and if you're about to prudishly sneer at me for being a perverse viewer then I suggest you really examine your own viewing habits first.)

I've had a few different phases throughout the last year or so, getting way too into a number of different objects of desire, but most recently my fixation has been latched firmly and intensely onto the film career of Elliott Gould between 1969 and 1974. My interest in his career evaporates immediately after 1974, and I haven't bothered with the few bit-parts he had before 1969, but otherwise I've sought out and sat through all of his work from this period.

If you watch all twelve feature films from the first five years of Elliott Gould's cinematic career, starting with Paul Marzusky's Bob & Alice & Ted & Carol (1969) and ending with Robert Altman's California Split (1974)—as I have just spent the last week or so doing, going out of my way to track down the more obscure films in shitty low-quality VHS rips—you will see a lot of flesh. Most of the films from this period of Elliott Gould's career are sex comedies and most of them give him—as well as the various women he is seducing or being seduced by in these films—at least one opportunity to disrobe. He often puts on a pair of pyjamas, sky blue or salmon pink, which he wears while arguing with someone in bed before either having or failing to have sex. (Pyjamas perform a particular function in the sex comedy genre that I haven't figured out—something to do with foreplay and frustration.) The image has stayed in my mind of Elliott Gould in Bob & Carol & Ted & Alice, wearing his blue PJs, running on the spot to burn off some excess energy after getting stoned, with the bottom button on his pyjama jacket undone so a triangle of hair and skin is tantalisingly visible, his lower stomach, from his waistband to his navel. In some of his films from this period (especially Stuart Rosenberg's Move, a subpar and vaguely surrealist comedy about the difficulties of finding a reliable removals service in New York City, from 1970) Elliott Gould gets undressed about once every ten minutes—maybe even more than that. Sometimes he just strips down to his underwear, which is usually an unflattering pair of large white briefs, as was the style at the time, but sometimes he takes everything off, and slips under some bedsheets or into a bath before the camera is permitted any suggestive glimpses of what's going on below his waist—again, the strange chasteness demanded by the generic conventions of the sex comedy: plenty of bare breasts on display, but little else.

Elliott Gould is a tall guy, somewhere over six foot, and he's also a big man. If Elliott Gould had been a star in the fifties (not that he'd have been allowed—he's too excessive in his performances, he's too neurotic, in other words too Jewish for 1950s Hollywood), he'd have fallen into the masculine category of the beefcake, and would possibly have been compared to someone like Rock Hudson—but Rock Hudson's career was built on the perfect almost-hairlessness of his enormous torso, his non-threatening hygiene, whereas Elliott Gould is a hirsute man, with a lot of back hair, and as often as not sporting a Zapata moustache. There's an essay from the early 90s called "Rock Hudson's Body", written by the art historian Richard Meyer, which describes the ways that the constructed image of Rock Hudson as a sexually-passive gentle giant effectively sanitised and made acceptable the erotic charge that viewers (both female and male) got from looking at his preposterously large body (deliberately shot to seem to exceed the frame) in his movies and publicity photos, all in aid of the production of a clean and pure heterosexuality untainted by the messiness of any actual fucking. The irony of this, as Meyer points out, is that this sanitary straightness was concocted by a publicity machine largely consisting of gay men (Rock Hudson's manager and agent, Henry Wilson, in particular), and the very site of this desirable cleanliness was the body of man who also preferred sleeping with men. (The open secret of Rock Hudson's own sexuality was covered up in his heyday by a three-year lavender marriage to Phyllis Gates, which worked well enough until he went public with his AIDS diagnosis in the 80s.) Rock Hudson's body is a useful demonstration of how queer male erotic fantasies can saturate popular culture and our collective imaginations, for men and women, straight or not, even when they aren't ever made explicit—or, in the case of Rock, are explicitly denied.

But Elliott Gould 1969–1974 is not really like Rock Hudson, a passive hunk onto which the viewer's desire is safely projected and contained; a man who is allowed a chaste on-screen kiss now and then, but who is more often than not the pursued rather than the pursuer. Rock Hudson does not fuck, but Elliott Gould 1969–1974 certainly fucks. At least, for the most part he does; at least, sex is a concern for him, in a way that it never was allowed to be for Rock. In his films, Elliott Gould 1969–1974 is almost always a highly sexualised figure: his career fully takes off in years of cultural promiscuity and a lot of his movies from this time are about adultery: films about the bourgeoisie dabbling with wife swapping, or neurotics getting off the couch and into bed. Fresh from his divorce from Barbra Streisand, Elliott Gould 1969–1974 either has a lot of sex in his films or he is surrounded by beautiful women who want to have sex with him despite his refusals. In 1970, annus mirabilis, he was the lead in four films, and was one of the biggest names in the movies: this fame is itself a kind of virility. Up until he worked with Ingmar Bergman on The Touch in 1971, Elliott Gould spends his films sleeping with either his wife or girlfriend or other people's wives and girlfriends. Then his career is somehow ruined by Bergman and he gets too big for his boots perhaps: he hits a wall by acting erratically during the production of A Glimpse of Tiger (eventually made as What's Up, Doc? by Peter Bogdanovich, starring none other than Barbra Streisand in the part Gould was supposed to play), and he goes away and has psychoanalysis for a couple of years, before returning to the screen in a more chaste and erotically detached mode.

At this point in his career, even if he's pursued or has the opportunity to fool around with someone, no strings attached, Elliott Gould 1969–1974 generally turns them down. It so happens that these denials of his former sexual excesses usually take place in his better films, especially two of those he made with Robert Altman: The Long Goodbye, in which he lives next door to a bunch of young women with a taste for doing naked yoga on their balconies, where he's just a respectful and good neighbour to them, a guy who buys them brownie mix and doesn't bat an eyelid at all that exposed and tanned skin; and California Split, in which he lives with two sex workers with hearts of gold, with whom he pals around and is mothered by—but the relationship seems not to have even a remote tang of the erotic, and he prefers spending his time involved in an elaborate seduction of George Segal. These films are more aggressively homosocial than his earlier work, with the exceptions of M*A*S*H and Bob & Carol & Ted & Alice: they are transparently about men wanting to hang out with each other, to the sometimes intentional and sometimes unintentional exclusion of women. In psychoanalysis a no is often a yes. Elliott Gould 1969–1974 often is saying no to the women and yes to the men. This might be to do with Robert Altman's misogyny as much as it's anything to do with Elliott Gould 1969–1974 himself, but it's also—for better or worse—part of where my fantasies take over: when I watch California Split, I don't want to be Elliott Gould. I want to be George Segal, inundated and dazzled by Elliott Gould's charisma and charm and energy and humour. I want to go to the bar with him and then for us to wind up back at his apartment.

Elliott Gould 1969–1974 is straight. That seems pretty obvious, and also has to be more or less taken for granted, since there was effectively no scope for explicitly acknowledged same-sex male desire in the masculinist just-guys-being-dudes American cinema of the early 1970s; a period of filmmaking which seems particularly concerned with men trying to figure out what kind of relationships they can have with each other in the disillusioned and cynical years after the utopian impulses of the 1960s had hardened and crumbled. Despite being a part of "New Hollywood" (and its turn away from the figure of the star and the studio system and towards the director), Elliott Gould 1969–1974 is a star in the classic sense of the word, and as such always seems to play himself in these movies. It doesn't matter what film you watch, you're watching Elliott Gould. He said as much in interviews; there's no method acting here, he just turns up to set and is himself. His characters are straight and they just like hanging out with other guys; sports are important for him, particularly basketball—the perpetually sanctioned realm of expressive homosociality.

Personally, I don't care about sports and I've got no illusions that Elliott Gould 1969–1974 and I are going to grab a few beers and then maybe, if things go well, we'll end up back at his apartment and start fooling around. But surely this is what cinema is for, and what it's always been for: fantasy. It's about the construction of ego-ideals (I want to be Elliott Gould 1969–1974) and about allowing ourselves to be surprised by our desire, and then perhaps to understand it better (I want to fuck or be fucked by Elliott Gould 1969–1974). Films are not a good guide to life, or to human nature and behaviour, or to the questions of what we should do and who we should be while we do it, but nevertheless that's what we use them for. In a time when our access to other people is scarce and fraught with risk and uncertainty, the cinephilic fixation gives us something that we don't get in many other places—a way of trying to answer those crucial questions: what is it that I want? And who is it that I want it from?

PS A CHRONOLOGICAL LIST OF ELLIOTT GOULD FILMS 1969–1974

Bob & Carol & Ted & Alice (1969): wife swapping Los Angeles comedy featuring E.G. as the straightest laced member of a bourgeois friendship group dabbling with unfree late 60s freedoms. M*A*S*H (1970): cynical buddy comedy set in a military hospital during the Korean War; E.G. at an extreme of furious zaniness. Getting Straight (1970): Vietnam/West Coast campus comedy starring E.G. as a grad student and veteran trying to get teaching qualification and failing to stay out of the protests; the only cinematic depiction I've seen of a US grad school oral qualifying exam in English Literature. Move (1970): surrealist New York comedy about E.G. (playing a part-time dog walker and pornography ghostwriter) trying to move apartment while regularly dissociating into a fantasy world. I Love My Wife (1970): cynical adultery comedy, featuring E.G. as a successful surgeon who becomes increasingly dissatisfied with his life and sleeps around out of boredom and hollow ambition. Little Murders (1971): cynical neurotic New York black comedy about the hollowness of contemporary life in a city riddled with meaningless violence, with E.G. as a passive man drifting into deeper futility, redeemed by succumbing to homicidal urges. The Touch (1971): E.G. goes to Sweden to work with Ingmar Bergman on a miserable adultery drama which is also obliquely about generational trauma and the Holocaust; E.G.'s most serious and most explicitly Jewish role, which also maybe led to him having a small breakdown. A couple of years off while he has the breakdown, before returning to do The Long Goodbye (1973): cynical drifting Los Angeles noir deflating the mythology of Humphrey Bogart, with E.G. as an orally fixated wise-acre who sweats his way through a black suit in the blazing sun—easily a career highlight. Busting (1974): cynical/gritty Los Angeles buddy cop movie about the Vice Squad, quite grimly homophobic and hollow; E.G. appears opposite Robert Blake, an actor who would later be murkily involved in killing his wife. Who? (1974): dreary and boring Cold War sci-fi spy thriller; E.G. looks absolutely incensed that he's been reduced to this and doesn't put in any effort at all. California Split (1974): cynical and deeply homosocial Los Angeles buddy comedy about the hollowness of gambling addiction, with E.G. opposite George Segal; as with The Long Goodbye (also directed by Robert Altman) E.G. is truly at his best here; one of the very few actually good films from this period in his career.

Drawn

When the eye sees a thing
of beauty it wants to draw
closer now

Where dawn enters the mouth
curved through a jagged rock
carved face

When we spotted the horses
two, drew near, knew breath
drew blood

Where deep in the obsidian
eyed glint of a swift animal
desire rose

When our throats slaked those
vermilion borders stained with
madder lake

Where we marked out hide
soft bruised and pelted raw
blushed rivulets

When light falls to an eye
flayed by beauty then, yes
then again

Author's note: This poem references the dappled horses cave painting at la Grotte du Pech Merle. Its first line opens a dialogue with Ludwig Wittgenstein, who once wrote: when the eye sees a thing of beauty, the hand wants to draw it.

There Is A Man

Even water buffaloes dream. In their creation myth,

the white bird brings down the sky like rain

in her digits. And the sun just keeps rising forever.

For the egrets, the great water buffalo, like a workhorse,

drags up the ground from the water so they can land.

Clearly cows are in communication with something

divine. Everything that bathes and wallows, even in mud,

commands an inner life. Underwater light is visible

as tractor beams, pulling up. In the air its true nature disappears.

There's a reason gods come down as animals so I'm doubtful we invented belief.

Elephants adorn the dead, chimpanzees dance for heavy rainfall.

Every one has a language, the failure is ours. It is not only biology

why the buffalo taxis the bird around the waterways.

I could argue against human exceptionalism but

even in this title, there is a man. At the end of the world

the egret pulls the sky down again, and there is darkness.

But what do men know of the world without men?

Acknowledgements

Gratitude to the friends and collaborators who contributed to this book and to those who've contributed to the Lugubriations Substack. Subscribe at lugubriations.substack.com

Special thanks to Theo Inglis our cover designer, and to Aaron Kent our publisher.

Onwards.
— Roisin Agnew.

LAY OUT YOUR UNREST

CPSIA information can be obtained
at www.ICGtesting.com
Printed in the USA
BVHW040732230722
642850BV00005B/855

9 781915 079794